Fingerpower® FUN

Level Four

Compiled, edited and arranged by Jeff Schaum

FOREWORD

The purpose of these pieces is to provide musical experiences beyond the traditional Fingerpower® books. The series offers students fun-to-play melodies which have many technic benefits. The pieces are arranged in order of progressive difficulty and nicely supplement all method books at this level.

A planned variety key signatures, time signatures, syncopations, dynamics, phrase groups and use of staccato helps develop basic musicianship. Any of the pieces would be ideal for recital or school performance.

A short technic preparatory drill ("Finger Workout") focuses on some of the melodic patterns found in each piece.

INDEX

Schaum Publications, Inc.
10235 N. Port Washington Rd. • Mequon, WI 53092 • www.schaumpiano.net

© Copyright 2013, 1983 and 1969 by Schaum Publications, Inc., Mequon, Wisconsin • International Copyright Secured
All Rights Reserved • Printed in U.S.A.
ISBN-13: 978-1-936098-90-3

Finger Workout: Play this exercise five times daily as a warm-up for "L.H. Bounce."

L.H. Bounce

Moderato ♩ = 108 - 112 *(swing 8ths)*

Jeff Schaum

3

4

Finger Workout: Play this exercise five times daily as a warm-up for "Wind Sprints."

Wind Sprints

Allegro ♩ = 80 - 92

Jeff Schaum

Catching your breath.

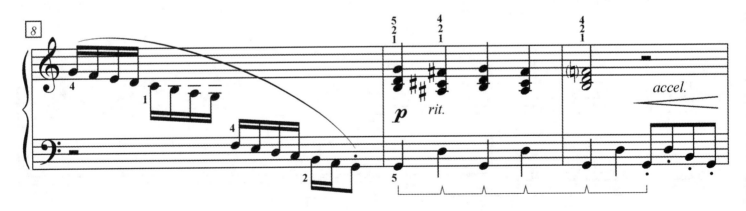

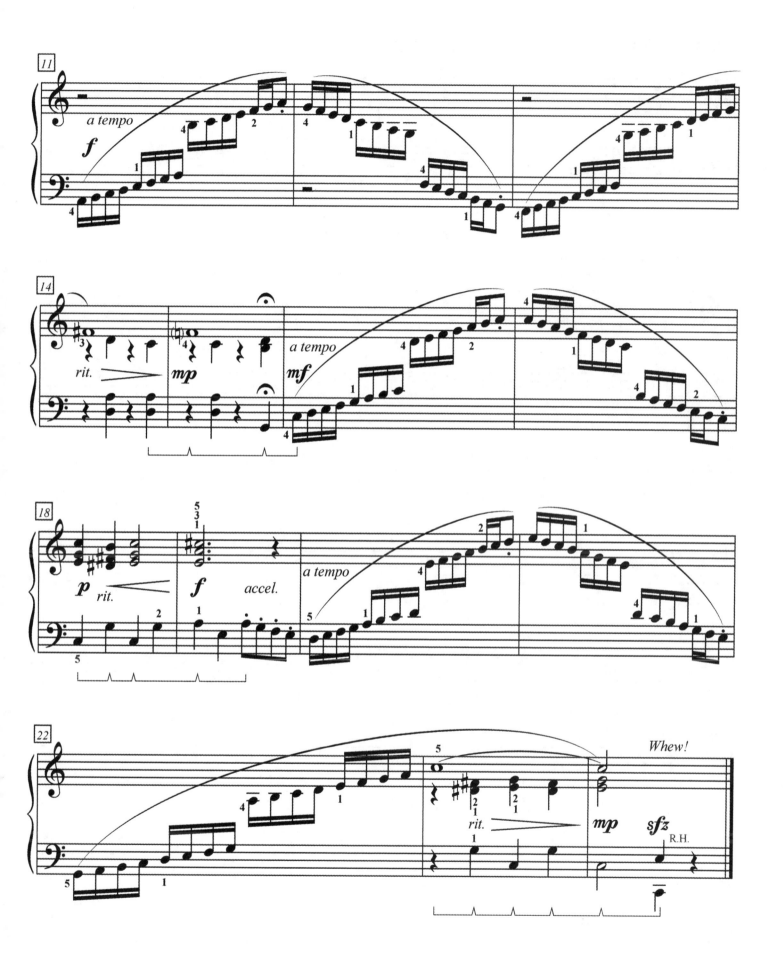

Finger Workout: Play this exercise five times daily as a warm-up for "Hopscotch."

Hopscotch

Elizabeth Gest
Jeff Schaum

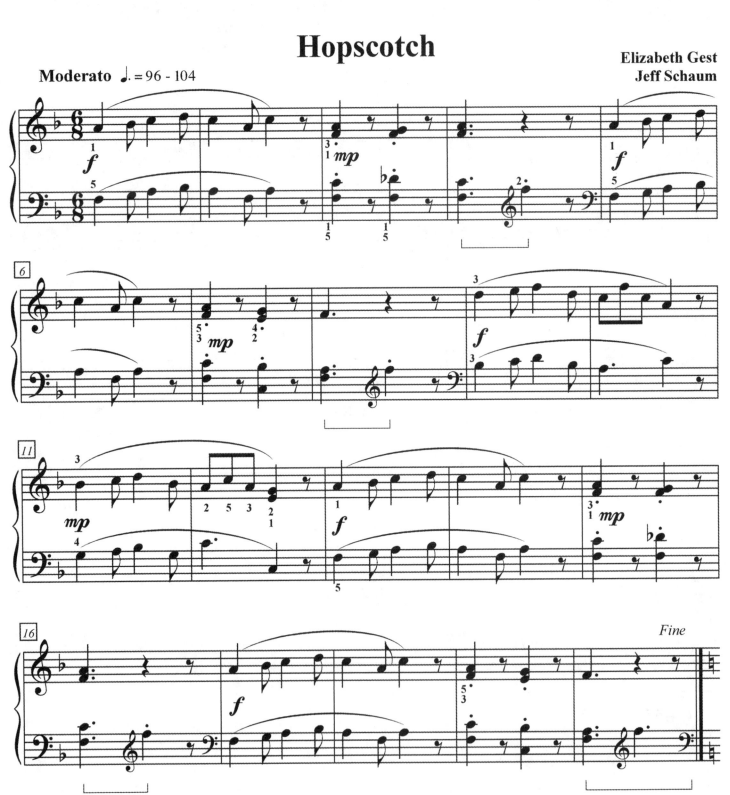

8

Finger Workout: Play this exercise five times daily as a warm-up for "Rainfall."

Rainfall

Larghetto ♩ = 60

Jeff Schaum

Finger Workout: Play this exercise five times daily as a warm-up for "Royal March."

Royal March

Kevin E. Cray

Finger Workout: Play this exercise five times daily as a warm-up for "Leaves In The River."

Leaves In The River

Larghetto ♩ = 56 - 62

Jeff Schaum

13

Finger Workout: Play this exercise five times daily as a warm-up for "Nifty Fifty."

Nifty Fifty

Andante ♩. = 84 - 92

Jeff Schaum

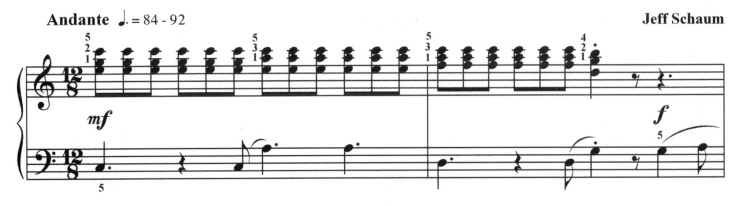

Finger Workout: Play this exercise five times daily as a warm-up for "Jumpin' Rope."

Jumpin' Rope

Allegro ♩. = 96 - 104

Jeff Schaum

18

Finger Workout: Play this exercise five times daily as a warm-up for "Secrets."

Secrets

Jeff Schaum

Finger Workout: Play this exercise five times daily as a warm-up for "Vacation Day."

Vacation Day

Jeff Schaum

Moderato ♩. = 100 - 108

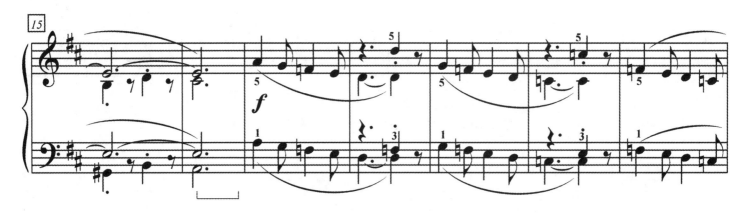

Finger Workout: Play this exercise five times daily as a warm-up for "Silent Movie."

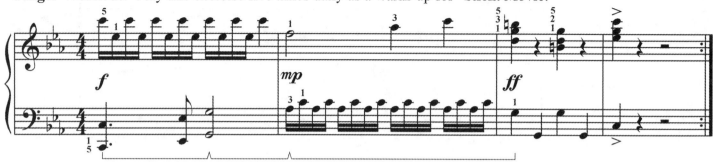

Silent Movie

Andante ♩ = 72 - 84

Jeff Schaum

The villian delights in the capture of the innocent lass!

The damsel in distress cries out:
"Will someone please save me?!"

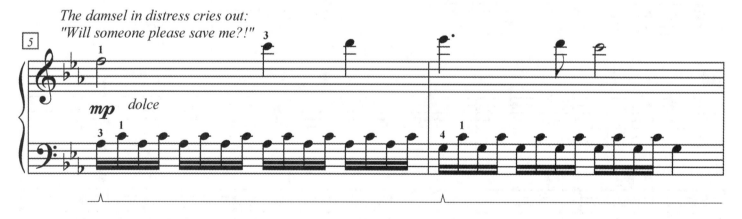